W9-AQV-201

TRAVEL WITH THE GREAT EXPLORERS

Explore with

Christopher Columbus

Cynthia O'Brien

Crabtree Publishing Company

www.crabtreebooks.com

Crabtree Publishing Company
www.crabtreebooks.com

Author: Cynthia O'Brien
Publishing plan research and development:
  Reagan Miller
Managing editor: Tim Cooke
Editorial director: Lindsey Lowe
Editors: Kelly Spence, Natalie Hyde
Proofreader: Kathy Middleton
Designer: Lynne Lennon
Picture manager: Sophie Mortimer
Design manager: Keith Davis
Children's publisher: Anne O'Daly
Production coordinator
  and prepress technican: Tammy McGarr
Print coordinator: Margaret Amy Salter

Produced by Brown Bear Books for
  Crabtree Publishing Company

Photographs:
Front Cover: Art Archive: Museo de la Torre del Oro
Seville/Dagli Orti cr; **Robert Hunt Library:** Metropolitan
Museum of Art main; **Shutterstock:** Knumina Studios br;
Topfoto: The Granger Collecction tr.

Interior: Alamy: Glasshouse Images 19, North Wind Picture
Archives 22tr; **Art Archive:** Christopher Columbus Birthplace
Valladolid/Dagli Orti 29b, Museo de la Torre del Oro
Seville/Dagli Orti 9t, 13, Navel Museum Genoa/Dagli Orti 8;
Editado por Henry of Mainz: 15t; **Library of Congress:** 6-7,
23c; **Mary Evans Picture Library:** 18, 20, 21cr, Everett
Collection 21b, Interfoto/Sammlung Rauch 18-19, The National
Archives, London, England 16; **Robert Hunt Library:** 7
Metropolitan Museum of Art 6; **Shutterstock:** 16-17, Christian
Draghici 24t, Yuttasak Jannarong 22bl, Knumina Studios 24b,
Andrew Zarivny 23br; **Thinkstock:** AbleStock 11tl, Dorling
Kindersley 12, 14, istockphoto 11b, 29tl; **Topfoto:** ClassicStock
27, The Granger Collection 9b, 10, 15b, 17, 25, 26, 28

Library and Archives Canada Cataloguing in Publication

O'Brien, Cynthia (Cynthia J.), author
    Explore with Christopher Columbus / Cynthia O'Brien.

(Travel with the great explorers)
Includes index.
Issued in print and electronic formats.
ISBN 978-0-7787-1245-9 (bound).--ISBN 978-0-7787-1257-2 (pbk.).--
ISBN 978-1-4271-7572-4 (pdf).--ISBN 978-1-4271-7568-7 (html)

    1. Columbus, Christopher--Juvenile literature. 2. Explorers--
America--Biography--Juvenile literature. 3. Explorers--Spain--
Biography--Juvenile literature. 4. America--Discovery and
exploration--Spanish--Juvenile literature. I. Title.

E111.O37 2014   j970.01'5092   C2013-908701-X
                                             C2013-908702-8

Library of Congress Cataloging-in-Publication Data

O'Brien, Cynthia (Cynthia J.)
  Explore with Christopher Columbus / Cynthia O'Brien.
      pages cm. -- (Travel with the great explorers)
  Includes index.
  ISBN 978-0-7787-1245-9 (reinforced library binding) -- ISBN 978-0-
7787-1257-2 (pbk.) -- ISBN 978-1-4271-7572-4 (electronic pdf) -- ISBN
978-1-4271-7568-7 (electronic html)
  1. Columbus, Christopher--Juvenile literature. 2. Explorers--America--
Biography--Juvenile literature. 3. Explorers--Spain--Biography--
Juvenile literature. 4. America--Discovery and exploration--Spanish--
Juvenile literature. I. Title.

  E111.O14 2014
  970.01'5092--dc23
  [B]
                                             2013050816

Crabtree Publishing Company

Printed in Canada/022014/MA20131220

www.crabtreebooks.com 1-800-387-7650

Published in Canada
Crabtree Publishing
616 Welland Ave.
St. Catharines, ON
L2M 5V6

Published in the United States
Crabtree Publishing
PMB 59051
350 Fifth Avenue, 59th Floor
New York, New York 10118

Published in the United Kingdom
Crabtree Publishing
Maritime House
Basin Road North, Hove
BN41 1WR

Published in Australia
Crabtree Publishing
3 Charles Street
Coburg North
VIC, 3058

CONTENTS

Meet the Boss	4
Where Are We Heading?	6
Columbus' Voyages to the New World	8
Meet the Crew	10
Check Out the Ride	12
Solve It with Science	14
Hanging at Home	16
Meeting and Greeting	18
How to Lose Friends	20
I Love Nature	22
Fortune Hunting	24
This Isn't What It Said in the Brochure	26
End of the Road	28
Glossary & Timeline	30
On the Web & Books	31
Index	32

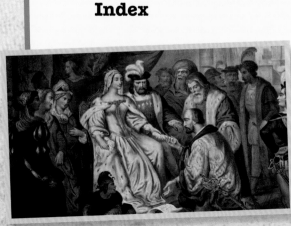

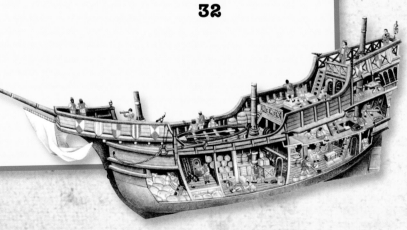

Meet the Boss

Did you know?

Columbus nearly died in 1476 when the merchant ship he was on was attacked by privateers. Columbus swam ashore in Portugal—where he met his future wife!

In 1451, Christopher Columbus was born Cristoforo Colombo in Genoa, Italy. His birthplace was a busy port, and Columbus was drawn to the sea at an early age.

TRADESMAN'S SON

+ Learning the ropes

Columbus' father, Domenico, was a weaver. Later, he worked as a wool merchant. Columbus learned weaving from his father, but went to sea as a trader when he was a teenager. Columbus traveled across the Mediterranean and Aegean Seas, learning how to **navigate** and **pilot** a ship. After his ship was wrecked in 1476, Columbus moved to Lisbon, Portugal.

FRIENDS IN HIGH PLACES

☛ **Columbus marries in Portugal**

☛ **Royal connections open doors**

In 1479, Columbus married a noblewoman, Felipa Perestrello e Moniz. It was an important marriage for a navigator with such a humble background. Felipa's connections provided Columbus with the opportunity to meet other nobles, and even royalty! He spoke to King John II of Portugal about his plan to sail west to China. The King rejected the idea. Columbus decided to go to Spain to try his luck with King Ferdinand and Queen Isabella.

SHOW ME THE MONEY

★ **Campaign for cash**

★ **Convincing the committee**

Columbus was sure he could find a way to the **Spice Islands** of Asia if he traveled west. He named his plan the "Enterprise of the Indies." Columbus and his brother Bartholomew tried to raise money in Portugal, France, England, and Spain for their voyage. Only Ferdinand and Isabella of Spain took them seriously. They assigned a committee to review his plan. Twice the committee rejected it. But after six years of debate, the monarchs agreed to fund the voyage. If Columbus claimed land for Spain, he would share in the profits. He would also be given the title "Admiral of the Ocean Seas."

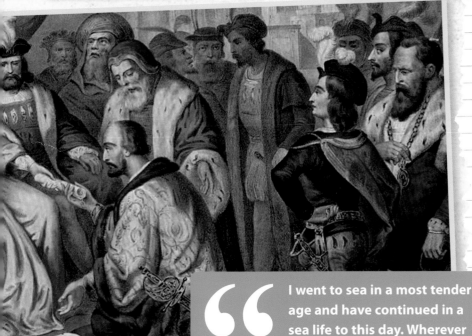

> "I went to sea in a most tender age and have continued in a sea life to this day. Wherever anyone has sailed, there have I sailed."
> *Columbus recalls his life as a sailor, 40 years after going to sea.*

My Explorer Journal

★ **Columbus spent years in royal courts around Europe, trying to get someone to pay for his expedition. Put yourself in Columbus' shoes. Write a letter of your own to Ferdinand and Isabella persuading them that it would be worthwhile to sail west to reach the Spice Islands of Asia.**

Where Are We Heading?

Christopher Columbus paved the way for Spanish settlement in the Caribbean and South America. Altogether, Columbus made four voyages on behalf of Ferdinand and Isabella of Spain.

Passage

Once Columbus discovered America, Europeans hoped a "Northwest Passage" would lead around or through it. The route would have made it easier to trade with Asia.

TRAVEL UPDATE

Spice Islands, here we come!

★Europeans knew that eastern lands, such as China, offered many riches. The overland trade route through Asia was called the Silk Road. It was long and difficult to travel. The **Ottoman Empire** blocked the route. Portuguese sailors searched for a route around Africa. Columbus was convinced that he could reach China, India, and Japan by sailing west.

LAND AHEAD!

☛ **Tired sailors drop anchor**

☛ **Aboriginal people welcome sailors**

After five weeks at sea, Columbus and his crew finally reached land on October 12, 1492. Columbus named the island San Salvador, which means Holy Savior. The native Taíno people who lived there called the island Guanahani. Columbus thought he had reached Asia like he had planned. In fact, he had only reached the Caribbean. San Salvador is one of 700 islands now called the Bahamas.

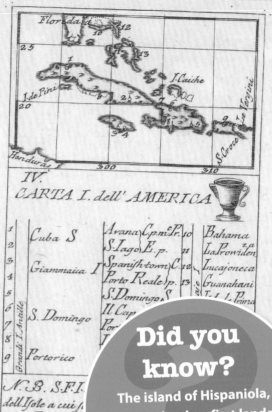

IS THIS JAPAN?

★ **The search for gold and spices**

★ **China must be nearby**

Beyond San Salvador, Columbus spotted more land. He named it Juana, after a Spanish prince. Today, this is Cuba. Columbus thought he had reached Cipangu, or what is now Japan. He wrote, "By the signs the Indians made of its greatness and of its gold and pearls, I thought that it must be the one — that is to say, Cipangu." Later, he decided Haiti was Japan, and Cuba was mainland China.

Did you know?

The island of Hispaniola, where Columbus first landed, is now divided between the countries of Haiti and the Dominican Republic.

GETTING SETTLED

+ Happy Christmas?

In December 1492, Columbus' ship the *Santa Maria* was wrecked off Hispaniola. On December 25, Columbus established *Villa de la Navidad*, or Christmas Town. When Columbus returned to Spain, he left 39 sailors behind. He ordered them to search for gold while he was gone.

ROUND TRIPS

☛ **Many islands explored**

☛ **Explorers exhausted**

Columbus made three more voyages across the Atlantic Ocean. He and his brothers founded settlements. One of these, Santa Domingo, became the first permanent city in the **New World**. On his third voyage, Columbus traveled to the coast of Venezuela and to Trinidad. His final voyage ended in Jamaica. By this time, he was sick and tired. He sailed back to Spain in 1504 and never returned to the New World.

COLUMBUS' VOYAGES TO THE NEW WORLD

Columbus traveled across the Atlantic Ocean to the New World on four voyages. He was determined to find the Northwest Passage and to claim fame and fortune for Spain, as well as himself.

NORTH AMERICA

San Salvador

Hispaniola

Cuba

CENTRAL AMERICA

Caribbean Sea

SOUTH AMERICA

San Salvador
After five weeks at sea on his first voyage, Columbus made **landfall** on San Salvador, a small island in what is now the Bahamas. He and his crew arrived there on October 12, 1492.

Cuba
After leaving San Salvador, Columbus sailed to the north coast of Cuba. Columbus believed he had arrived in China and sent men to locate the emperor. They failed, but visited a Taíno village instead.

Central America
Columbus visited Central America in 1502, on his fourth voyage. In Panama he learned from native people about another ocean to the west. It was the first time Europeans had heard of the Pacific Ocean.

Jamaica
On his fourth voyage, Columbus and his crew were **marooned** for over a year on what is now Jamaica after their ship was wrecked just offshore.

Hispaniola

Columbus landed on the island of Hispaniola on his first voyage. He founded a **colony** named La Navidad, which was later destroyed by the native people. On his second voyage, in 1494, Columbus founded two new settlements on the island, first at La Isabela and later at Santo Domingo.

ATLANTIC OCEAN

Spain

Cádiz

Columbus made his voyages to the New World on behalf of Spain. He set sail from and returned to the main Spanish port, Cádiz, which would become extremely wealthy thanks to trade with the Americas.

AFRICA

Orinoco

When Columbus visited the coast of Venezuela on his third voyage in 1498, he saw the mouth of the Orinoco River. He believed that due to of the size of the freshwater river, Venezuela was not just an island, but part of a whole continent: South America.

Key

—————▶	First voyage, 1492–93
·········▶	Second voyage, 1493–96
—————▶	Third voyage, 1498–1500
·········▶	Fourth voyage, 1502–04

Meet the Crew

Columbus traveled with many other navigators and explorers on his four voyages across the Atlantic. Some of those who sailed with him became famous explorers in their own right.

Mapmaker's Legacy

- ☛ Santa María's captain publishes map
- ☛ Map shows new continent!

Juan de la Cosa, a **cartographer** and navigator, owned Columbus' **flagship**, the *Santa Maria*. He traveled on Columbus' first two voyages across the Atlantic. In 1499, de la Cosa sailed to Venezuela with European explorers Amerigo Vespucci and Alonso de Ojeda. De la Cosa's map, published in 1500, was the first European map to show the New World.

Map

Juan de la Cosa drew the New World on a map in 1500. It was first called America by another mapmaker in 1507.

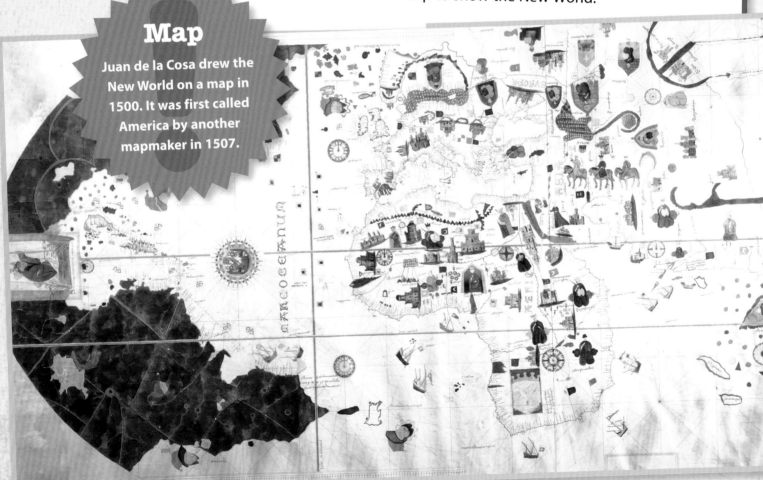

EACH MAN FOR HIMSELF

★ **Captain goes solo**

★ **Independent-minded brothers**

The Pinzón brothers, Martín and Vicente, traveled with Columbus on his first voyage. Martín commanded the *Pinta*, and his brother, Vincente, the *Niña*. Not long after they reached the Caribbean, Martín left to explore on his own. That made Columbus angry. Martín rejoined Columbus later, but again took the *Pinta* **off course** on its way home. His brother, Vincente, became an explorer. In 1499, he traveled to the coasts of Venezuela and Brazil.

Did you know?

Martín Pinzón was so confident about Columbus' plan to sail west that he funded a third of the cost of the expedition.

King and Queen Ban Jews

☞ **Converts board ship**

☞ **Which way to the Khan's palace?**

Ferdinand and Isabella issued the Alhambra Decree in 1492. It banned all Jews from Spain. At least seven Jewish men joined Columbus' expedition. Among them were Luis de Torres, an interpreter, and Maestre Bernal, a doctor. When Columbus landed in Cuba, which he thought was China, he sent de Torres to find the palace of China's emperor, the Khan. De Torres found only villages. Both de Torres and Bernal stayed on in the Caribbean to begin a new life in the New World.

KEEP IT IN THE FAMILY

+ **Like father, like son**

Columbus had two sons, Diego and Ferdinand. After his father's death, Diego became **governor** of Columbus' colony on Hispaniola. Ferdinand sailed with his father on his fourth voyage, later writing a book about Columbus' life and travels.

Check Out the Ride

By the late 1400s, European shipbuilders had made great advances. Sailors, traders, and explorers needed sturdy vessels to take them into unknown, dangerous waters.

Ships Wanted!

☞ Royal debts paid

☞ Columbus secures ships

The Spanish king and queen paid for the crew and supplies that Columbus needed for his voyage. To raise money, the Royal Court put pressure on the town of Palos to repay their debts to Spain. In order to pay it, two citizens of Palos each gave Columbus a ship. He hired a third, and was ready to go.

LEADER OF THE GANG

+ Columbus chooses flagship

The *Santa María* was the largest of Columbus' ships. He rented it from Juan de la Cosa. The *Santa María* was a **carrack**, or *nao*, with five sails on its three masts. Columbus thought the *Santa María* was clumsy and slow. However, it was a strong and sturdy ship. It was built to carry cargo and a large crew.

Cargo

A carrack was built with maximum storage space so the ship could carry as much cargo as possible. This made a voyage more profitable.

STORMY SEAS AHEAD

The Atlantic Ocean and Caribbean Sea are subject to fierce storms. Sailors needed ships that could stand up to rough seas and strong winds. The small Portuguese caravel was an ideal vessel, and also sailed well in shallow coastal waters. Both the *Pinta* and the *Niña* were caravels. At Columbus' request, both had square sails on their main and foremasts. A lateen, or triangular sail, was added on the third mast to help with tacking, or sailing into the wind.

> "I determined to count less than the true distance, that the crew might be dismayed if the voyage should prove long." *Columbus describes how he falsified the ship's log.*

Did you know?

Of the three ships on his first voyage, Columbus' favorite was the *Niña*. It was the smallest, but it was also the quickest.

TRAVEL UPDATE

Island travel

★The native Taíno people moved around the islands of the Caribbean in canoes, called *canoas*. They hollowed out tree trunks using sharp stones. The canoes were quick and efficient. They varied in size, but, Columbus wrote, "they are not so wide, because they are made of a single log of timber." He saw some canoes carrying as many as 80 rowers. The Taíno chiefs owned these larger canoes while fishermen used smaller boats.

Solve it with Science

Columbus navigated by using charts, maps, and wind patterns. He was the first sailor to use the trade winds to sail swiftly to and from the New World.

Big Pear

After years of observations at sea, Columbus came to the conclusion that Earth was not round, like a ball, but was shaped more like a pear.

SEA OF DARKNESS

☛ Pioneering prince

☛ School for navigators opens

In the 1400s, sailors were frightened to explore the Atlantic Ocean. They called it the "Sea of Darkness." But a Portuguese prince named Henry the Navigator began training sailors and funding exploration in the 1420s. The Portuguese discovered the trade winds. These are winds that cross the Atlantic in wide bands, one blowing mainly from east to west, the other from west to east. They helped Columbus sail to the New World and then return home again.

CHANGING DIRECTION

★ Compass points the way!

★ That's not the North!

On his first voyage across the Atlantic, Columbus knew about compass variation. This means that a compass points to the magnetic north, not the true north (or North Pole). However, as he sailed west, Columbus noticed something. The variation was not constant. It changed as he traveled west. This observation helped him navigate his way across the ocean.

Did you know?

By the time Columbus began exploring, most people knew the Earth was round. This had been proven by the ancient Greeks.

DOING THE NUMBERS

+ Columbus studies Ptolemy and D'Ailly

An ancient Greek named Ptolemy believed that Earth was half land and half water. Columbus thought the ocean could not be that big. He read a book by Pierre d'Ailly called *Imago Mundi*, or Image of the World. D'Ailly believed the ocean was much smaller. Columbus decided he could reach Asia by traveling west only 2,700 nautical miles. In fact, this was not even halfway.

I RECKON WE'RE HERE

★ Old ways are the best ways

Under cloudy skies, early sailors navigated using a method called dead reckoning. Columbus used this method to determine a ship's position. He started with the ship's last location. Then he calculated the direction, speed, and time they had spent sailing. By doing this, Columbus soon found the ship's new position.

SEEING THE FUTURE

☛ Astronomy tables predict eclipse

☛ Admiral saves his crew

Columbus used **astronomy tables** when he was stranded on Jamaica. He figured out that an **eclipse** would occur on February 29, 1504. He told the Taíno that the moon would disappear forever if they did not give him food. The eclipse happened as Columbus predicted. The frightened Taíno begged him to return the moon in exchange for giving him all the food he wanted.

Hanging at Home

After such a long time at sea on their first voyage, Columbus and his men rejoiced when they spotted land. They saw a lush, green island covered with palm trees and flowers.

Scurvy

Scurvy is caused by a lack of Vitamin C. It causes bruising under the skin and makes the teeth fall out. It can be prevented by eating fruit, such as limes.

TRAVEL UPDATE

Close Quarters

★Sailors were not used to being at sea for extended periods without making landfall. Onboard, working hours were long. The men spent any spare time praying or singing. Most of the time, there was only dry crackers, called hardtack, to eat with salted meat and fish. There were few vegetables or fruit, so sailors sometimes developed a serious disease called scurvy. There was wine or water to drink. Most crew slept on the deck, wherever they could find a space. Only the captains and pilots slept in cabins—and they were tiny.

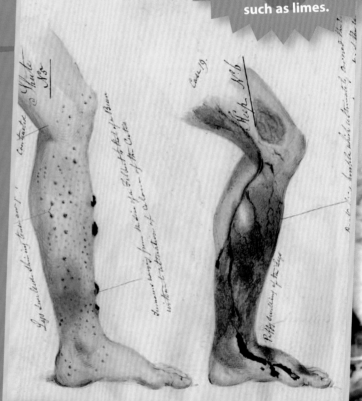

WE CALL IT HOME

★ **Columbus observes local culture**

★ **Has this potato got sugar on it?**

The Taíno people had never seen Europeans before Columbus landed. They welcomed their visitors with local foods the Europeans had not tried, such as sweet potatoes and cassava, a root vegetable. Columbus noticed their large homes were made of wooden poles, woven straw, and palm leaves. Many families shared one house. Inside, they slept on hammocks.

SETTLEMENT IN RUINS

☛ **Nothing but ashes**

☛ **No survivors**

Columbus returned to La Navidad in November 1493. The settlement and the nearby village of the native Arawak had been burned to the ground. All of the men Columbus had left behind a year earlier were dead. He and his crew discovered clothing and some remains.

> " Both men and women cried with loud voices 'Come and see the men who have come from the sky.'" *Columbus describes his welcome in Hispaniola.*

Did you know?

The Taíno women had to prepare the cassava root carefully. Otherwise, it could be poisonous.

My Explorer Journal

★ **Many of Columbus' crew wanted to sail home after weeks on the ocean with no sight of land. Use details in the text to make a list of reasons that the sailors might have given Columbus to explain their decision.**

Meeting and Greeting

Columbus called the people he met "los Indios." He thought he had landed in the Indies, in Asia. In fact, he had encountered the Caribbean people—the Taíno and the Carib.

Welcome, Strangers

- ☞ Taíno greet visitors
- ☞ Caciques control the kingdoms

The Taíno people lived on the Caribbean islands of Cuba, Jamaica, Hispaniola, and Puerto Rico, and on the coast of South America. Columbus met different groups of Taíno. He believed they were uncivilized, but they had a complex society. Chiefs called *caciques* led Taíno *caciquats*, or kingdoms. The caciques lived in large huts in the centers of their villages. Columbus was made a cacique himself as a sign of friendship.

WHAT WILL YOU GIVE ME?

- ★ Treasures for trinkets
- ★ Where's the gold?

The Lucayan tribe met Columbus as he landed. Like the other Taíno, they were traders. They exchanged goods with the European visitors. The Spanish sailors traded glass beads and other things for spun cotton and parrots. Columbus was more interested in the gold piercing the Lucayans' noses. He was sure there was more gold to find.

Did you know?

Columbus wrote to Spain that the people he met were so gentle it would be easy to force them to work for the Spanish.

SPANISH ALLIANCE

+ Arrows fired at ships

The Ciguayos, another Taíno group, did not welcome Columbus. They fired arrows at his ships. Columbus met with their chief, Guacanagari, and formed an alliance, or friendship. The chief allowed Columbus to build a settlement at La Navidad after the wreck of the *Santa María* in December 1492. But other Taíno caciques were more suspicious of Columbus. They were angry with Guacanagari for encouraging the Europeans to build settlements.

Escape

When Guacanagari refused to cooperate with the other caciques to fight Columbus, he had to flee and live in the mountains, where he died.

Neighbors at War

- Raids terrorize Taíno
- Women taken captive

The Carib lived in what is now the Lesser Antilles. Over many years, they crossed the Caribbean in canoes with sails to raid Taíno villages to the north. The warriors killed the Taíno men and kidnapped the women as slaves. Columbus met the Carib on his second voyage. The Spanish fleet arrived at Santa Cruz, now St. Croix. As they returned to their ships, Carib warriors attacked them, killing one Spaniard. The Spanish fought back and captured the Caribs.

How to Lose Friends

Although Columbus' early relations with the Taíno were good, they soon crumbled. The Taíno began to think that the Spaniards treated them harshly. Things began to turn sour.

REBEL LEADER

+ Cacique captured

+ Caonabo dies in shipwreck

La Navidad was destroyed by a cacique named Caonabo because the settlers mistreated his people. Caonabo killed the Spaniards and burned the settlement. After discovering the destroyed settlement, Columbus sent soldiers to capture Caonabo. Riding horses and using fierce dogs, the Spaniards easily defeated the Taíno. Caonabo was put on a ship headed for Spain, but died when it was wrecked on the journey.

Queen of the Taíno

☞ Friendship turns to war

☞ Celebrated composer hanged

Caonabo's wife, Anacaona, was cacique of another group of Taíno. She was a famous composer of native **ballads**. Anacaona and her brother ruled together. They were friendly to Columbus, but after the death of Caonabo, the Taíno began a long war against the Spaniards. Eventually the Spanish governor had Anacaona and her nobles arrested and executed.

GOLD HUNTERS

★ **There's gold in them there hills**

★ **First tax in the Americas**

In 1494, Alonso de Ojeda found three large nuggets of gold in the foothills of the mountains in the heart of Hispaniola. Columbus believed the Taíno were hiding yet more gold. He made them lead Spanish expeditions into the mountains to search. When the expeditions found nothing, Columbus imposed a tax on the Taíno. All adult men had to give the Spaniards gold, or they would be punished.

Tricked

One story says that de Ojeda took a cacique captive by saying that shackles, or handcuffs, were a type of royal dress so he would put them on.

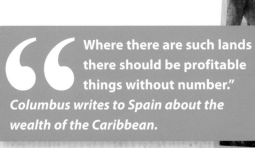

" Where there are such lands there should be profitable things without number."
Columbus writes to Spain about the wealth of the Caribbean.

★ **Imagine that you are Columbus. How could you persuade the Taíno to tell you where to find the best sources of gold?**

In Chains

☛ **Slaves sent to Spain**

When Columbus didn't find gold, he decided to make some money by selling slaves. In February 1495, he captured 1,500 Taíno. He sent 500 men and women to Spain. Not all of them survived the journey. He forced the rest into slavery. By the mid 1500s, only 200 or so Taíno survived.

I Love Nature

"I have never seen anything so beautiful," wrote Columbus of the Caribbean. He described the green trees and many flowers. The islands were full of other surprises, too.

Yummy

Peter Martyr, a 16th-century Spanish writer, said that iguana meat was as tasty as luxury meats in Europe, such as pheasant and peacock.

STRANGE CREATURES

- Thanks, but no thanks
- How about some turtle soup?

On his voyages, Columbus saw many new and strange animals. One was the **iguana**. The Taíno considered it a **delicacy**. The Spanish disagreed. In time, they tried the iguana meat and found they liked it. On his fourth voyage, Columbus saw another unusual sight. Strong winds blew his ship off course and he sailed to the Cayman Islands. He saw so many turtles there, he called the islands Las Tortugas, "the turtles."

COLORFUL TALKERS

- Parrots given to Queen
- Spanish admire green feathers

The Amazon parrot of South America, Mexico, and the Caribbean is rare today. But when Columbus first saw these parrots in 1492, he couldn't believe how many there were. "The flocks of parrots that darken the sun and the large and small birds of so many species are so different from our own that it is a wonder," he wrote. When he returned to Spain, he took a pair of the colorful birds as a gift for Queen Isabella.

LIGHT ONE FOR ME

+ New craze takes over Europe

Before 1492, Europeans had never heard of tobacco. This changed when Columbus and his men noticed the Taíno smoking. The Spanish watched as the Taíno lit small bundles of dried, fragrant leaves. The Taíno gave some leaves to the Spanish, who thought they were useless. Eventually, the sailors began to try smoking. They liked it so much that they brought dried leaves and seeds back to Spain. Before long, Europeans were smoking and chewing tobacco leaves. They didn't know it was bad for them.

My Explorer Journal

★ **Imagine you are Columbus. Write a letter describing a pineapple to someone who has never seen one before.**

Did you know?

The Europeans had never seen anyone smoking. Columbus wrote that the native people were "drinking the smoke" of herbs.

NEW ON THE MENU

☞ **A royal favorite**

☞ **Demand for pineapple**

In November 1493, Columbus and his crew landed on the island of Guadeloupe and went to explore. They found a deserted Carib village. Among the artifacts and human remains, they found fresh fruit and vegetables. A strange fruit caught their attention. They called it *piña* because it looked like a pinecone. It was a pineapple. Columbus took pineapples back as gifts for Queen Isabella. The queen was delighted with the sweet fruit and ordered Columbus to bring back more.

Fortune Hunting

In the 15th century, Europe's rulers and nobles realized the riches that lay in other lands. They sponsored expeditions to increase their wealth and power.

Spice it Up

☛ **Money to be made in spices**

☛ **New flavors come to Spain**

In the 15th century, Europeans could not get enough of spices. They loved pepper, nutmeg, and other exotic spices. This made spices very valuable. Columbus brought allspice, vanilla, and chili peppers back to Spain. The Spanish found these flavors fresh and exciting.

GOLDEN DREAM

+ **Gold rush comes to Hispaniola**

+ **New World set to boom**

Gold meant wealth and power. Columbus wanted both for himself and for Spain. In 1494, he built a small fort in central Hispaniola. He called it Concepción de la Vega. Today this is the town of La Vega in the Dominican Republic. Under Columbus' brother, Bartholomew, the fort grew. In 1508, the Spanish found gold nearby. Until the mid-1500s, so many Europeans came looking for gold that La Vega became the New World's first **boomtown**.

GREED TAKES OVER

★ **Taíno suffer under Spanish**

★ **Desperate measures taken**

Columbus was furious when his men failed to find gold on Hispaniola. The Spanish already used the Taíno as slaves. Now Columbus decided that they should also search for gold. He began a **tribute** system in which every three months, every Taíno over the age of 14 was to give Columbus gold in exchange for a token. If they did not receive a token, he punished them severely, sometimes having their hands cut off.

I BAPTIZE YOU...

★ **Spreading the Catholic faith**

King Ferdinand and Queen Isabella wanted everyone to be Catholic. One of Columbus' tasks was to convert native people he met. He wrote that, "It appears to me, that the people are ingenious, and would be good servants, and I am of the opinion that they would very readily become Christians, as they appear to have no religion." However, the Taíno did have their own beliefs. Converting them to Christianity was not easy or long-lasting.

"Your highnesses have another world here, from which such wealth can be drawn." *Columbus writes to Ferdinand and Isabella about America*

MOVING IN

☞ **Settlements grow**

☞ **A lasting legacy**

Columbus' brother, Bartholomew, founded La Nueva Isabela in 1496. In 1498, its official name became Santo Domingo. By the early 1500s, the colony was the gateway for the Spanish arriving in the New World. From here, they explored and settled on other Caribbean islands and in North and South America. Unlike Columbus' first two settlements, Santo Domingo lasted. Today it is the capital of the Dominican Republic.

This Isn't What It Said in the Brochure

Columbus dreamed of wealth and fame. These dreams did not include shipwrecks, murder, or prison. His adventures were to present him with all these challenges and more.

MUTINY ON THE ATLANTIC

☛ Sailors threaten revolt

After sailing for 70 days on his first voyage, Columbus' crew grew restless. Columbus did not want a **mutiny**, so he promised the sailors they would return home if they did not see land in two days. The next day they spotted San Salvador.

SHIPWRECK!

★ Santa María strikes coral reef

★ Flagship not seaworthy

On December 24, 1492, Columbus left Hispaniola for Spain. The crew had a party and fell asleep, leaving a cabin boy on watch. He was inexperienced and did not notice as the ship drifted off course. Not far from land, the current carried the Santa María into a **coral reef.** The reef destroyed the ship beyond repair. Columbus and his crew had to stay on the island a little longer than planned.

Did you know?

Columbus ordered his crew to take all the large timbers from the hull of the *Santa María*. He used them to build the settlement La Navidad.

Weather Forecast

STUCK IN THE DOLDRUMS

On Columbus' third voyage in 1498, his fleet was crossing the Atlantic when the sea fell calm and the wind disappeared. The ships floated helplessly for days. The crews were constantly thirsty in the hot sun, and nearly ran out of water. They had sailed into the Doldrums, an area with little wind near the equator. It took days for the wind to pick up again.

ISABELA FAILS

+ Settlement struggles

+ Poor location for crops

In 1493, Columbus founded a settlement on the north coast of Hispaniola called La Isabela. About 1,500 men settled there. They brought pigs, horses, and plants, but the European crops failed to grow. Men began fighting with each other and the Taíno. After five years, the Spanish abandoned La Isabela and established Santo Domingo.

Honor

Columbus named his settlement La Isabela in honor of the Spanish queen. Other explorers also named places they visited after the sponsors of their voyages.

CUFF HIM!

☞ Columbus arrested

When Ferdinand and Isabella heard tales of fighting at La Isabela, they sent Francisco de Bobadilla to investigate. He arrested Columbus and his brothers. He sent them back to Spain in chains. The monarchs appointed a new governor of Hispaniola. Columbus was furious.

TRAVEL UPDATE

Columbus stranded on island

★Long sea journeys and weather take their toll on ships. In June 1502, Columbus sailed to explore the coast of Central America. The ships did not make it home. Columbus and his men were stranded on Jamaica. They waited a year before they were rescued.

End of the Road

Columbus' fourth voyage to the New World was his last. He spent his last years in Spain. Sick and weak, Columbus fought for his rights to fame and fortune.

REMEMBER MY NAME

☛ Royal court ignores Columbus appeal

☛ Explorer falls from grace after arrest

Columbus was a favorite of Ferdinand and Isabella until he was arrested. Columbus felt cheated. He compiled the *Book of Privileges*. It listed the many promises that Columbus believed the crown had made and then broken. He wanted the rulers to restore the title he had lost in the colonies. He also wanted a share of the profits. Columbus' family continued to fight for these rights for years after his death.

PROS AND CONS

★ Disease devastates native people

★ Death sentence for the Taíno

Columbus brought European animals and plants to the New World. He brought Caribbean animals and plants to Europe. This is called the Columbian Exchange. But the Spanish also brought new diseases with them, such as measles and smallpox. The native people had no defenses against these diseases. Many Taíno became ill and died.

MAKE NO MISTAKE

+ Columbus unwilling to back down

Many people doubted that Columbus had reached Asia. Amerigo Vespucci and others decided that this New World was a new continent. Columbus himself never questioned his belief. Until his death, he maintained that he had sailed to Asia's outer islands. Just seven years later, Balboa traveled across Panama and saw the Pacific Ocean.

Ocean

When Vasco Nuñez de Balboa first saw the Pacific Ocean to the west of Panama, it was clear that another mighty ocean separated the New World from Asia.

My Explorer Journal

★ **Use details in the text to explain why Columbus was so convinced that he had found a route to Asia. What evidence did he have?**

" I came to serve you at the age of 28 and now I have not a hair on my head that is not white, and my body is infirm and exhausted." *Columbus complains about his treatment by the Spanish monarchs.*

A DISAPPOINTED MAN

☞ **Columbus dies at Valladolid**

☞ **Diego appointed governor of Hispaniola**

When Columbus returned to Spain in November 1504, he was very ill and in great pain. Queen Isabella died soon after he arrived. Columbus lost a great sponsor. King Ferdinand was not interested in the old traveler. Columbus spent time writing his *Book of Prophesies*. In it, he wrote bible passages and religious beliefs. Columbus died on May 20, 1506. He was 54 years old.

Did you know?

The explorer Amerigo Vespucci was the first man to suggest that America was not part of Asia, but a new continent. He eventually gave his name to the New World.

GLOSSARY

astronomy tables Charts that show the position of stars and other heavenly bodies at particular times of year

ballads Long poems that tell a story and are intended to be sung

boomtown A town that grows quickly; usually because of resources nearby

carrack A large sailing ship used to carry goods in the 15th and 16th centuries

cartographer Someone who studies and draws maps

colony A settlement or territory that is under the political control of a different country

coral reef A stony outcrop formed in shallow tropical waters by the hard remains of millions of tiny sea creatures

delicacy Something delightful or pleasing

eclipse An event in which the moon or an astronomical body such as a planet blocks the view of the sun from Earth

falsified To have changed information; to have misled

flagship The ship that carries the commander of a fleet

foremasts The masts closest to the front of ships

governor Someone who rules a colony or area on behalf of the monarch of a larger country

iguana A type of large lizard that lives in tropical America; it has spines on its back

landfall The land that is first seen or reached after a journey by sea or air

marooned To have put ashore and abandoned

merchant One who runs a business

mutiny A rebellion against someone in authority, especially by a ship's crew against their officers

navigate To plan and record the course of a journey

New World North and South America

off course Not following the intended route

Ottoman Empire A former empire made up of southeast Europe, western Asia, the Middle East, and parts of Africa

pilot A sailor who steers a vessel, often in dangerous waters

port A city, town, or other place where ships load or unload goods

privateers Pirate ships which sailed on behalf of a government during wartime

Spice Islands Islands located in Asia where Europeans traveled to trade for spices

tribute A payment made by one person or country to another

Columbus tries to find backers to pay for a voyage to Asia by sailing west across the Atlantic. He fails in England and Portugal.

OCTOBER 12
Columbus makes landfall in what is now the Bahamas. He goes on to explore Cuba and Hispaniola.

SEPTEMBER 25
Columbus leaves Cadiz, Spain, on his second voyage. He explores Hispaniola and founds a settlement in what is now Haiti.

1484 **1485** **1491** **1492** **1493**

Columbus moves to Spain to try to get backing for his voyage.

After six years of requests, King Ferdinand and Queen Isabella finally agree to support the voyage west.

AUGUST
Columbus sets sail from Spain with three ships.

MARCH 5
Columbus arrives back in Spain with news of the New World.

ON THE WEB

www.enchantedlearning.com/
explorers/page/c/columbus.shtml
Site about Columbus, with links to many
activities

http://video.nationalgeographic.co.uk
/video/kids/history-kids/christopher-
columbus-kids/
A video about Christopher Columbus produced
by National Geographic Kids History pages

http://pbsamerica.co.uk/christopher-
columbus
Video entitled The Magnificent Voyage of
Christopher Columbus

www.datesandevents.org/
people-timelines/15-christopher-
columbus-timeline.htm
Detailed timeline of Columbus' life and
achievements

BOOKS

Bodden, Valerie. *Columbus Reaches the New World* (Days of Change). Creative Education, 2009.

Feinstein, Stephen. *Opening Up the New World* (Great Explorers of the World). Enslow Publishing Co, 2009.

MacDonald, Fiona, and David Antram. *You Wouldn't Want to Sail with Christopher Columbus* (Famous Explorers). Franklin Watts, 2014.

Morganelli, Adrianna. *Christopher Columbus: Sailing to a New World* (In the Footsteps of Explorers). Crabtree Publishing, 2005.

Ollhoff, Jim. *Christopher Columbus* (Great Explorers). ABDO and Daughters, 2013.

West, David, and Jackie Gaff. *Christopher Columbus: The Life of a Master Navigator and Explorer* (Graphic Nonfiction). Rosen Publishing, 2005.

SEPTEMBER 29
Columbus returns to Spain.

AUGUST 24
Francisco de Bobadilla investigates rumors of misgovernment of Spanish colonies. He arrests Columbus and his brothers and sends them back to Spain in irons.

NOVEMBER 7
Columbus returns to Spain at the end of his final voyage.

1494   1498   1500   1502   1503   1504   1506

MAY 30
Columbus leaves Spain on his third voyage, on which he visits the coast of South America.

MAY 11
Having been restored to his position after his arrest, Columbus leaves Spain on his fourth voyage. He visits Honduras and Panama.

JUNE 25
Columbus is shipwrecked off Jamaica, and waits a year to be rescued.

MAY 20
Columbus dies peacefully at the Spanish court at Valladolid.

INDEX

A

Anacaona 20

astronomy tables 15

Atlantic Ocean 13, 14

B

Bahamas 6, 8

Balboa, Vasco Nuñez de 29

Bernal, Maestre 11

Bobadilla, Francisco de 27

Book of Privileges 28

Book of Prophesies 29

C

canoes 13

Caonabo 20

caravel 13

Caribbean Sea 9, 13, 18, 19

carrack 12

cassava 16, 17

China 11

Cipangu (Japan) 11

Columbian Exchange 28

Columbus, Bartholomew 5, 24, 25

compass 14

Cuba 8, 11

D

d'Ailly, Pierre 15

de la Cosa, Juan 10, 12

dead reckoning 15

Doldrums 27

Dominican Republic 25

E

eclipse 15

Enterprise of the Indies 7

F

Ferdinand, King 6, 7, 9, 25, 28, 29

foods 16, 22, 24

G

gold 18, 21, 24, 25

Guacanagari 19

H

Henry the Navigator 14

Hispaniola 5, 9, 11, 21, 24, 25, 26

I

iguana 22

Isabella, Queen 6, 7, 9, 22, 25, 28, 29

J

Jamaica 4, 11, 15, 27

Jews 11

L

La Isabela 27

La Navidad 11, 17, 19, 20, 26

M

map 8-9

mapping 8

N

native peoples 18–21

navigation 14–15

Niña 9, 13

O

Ojeda, Alonso de 21

Orinoco River 9

P

Pacific Ocean 29

parrot 22

Perestrello e Moniz, Felipa 4

Pinta 11, 13

Pinzón brothers 11

plants and animals 22–23, 28

Ptolemy 15

R

religion 25

S

San Salvador 6, 7, 8, 26

Santa Maria 7, 10, 26

Santo Domingo 11, 25, 27

scurvy 16

shipping 12–13

slavery 21, 25

spices 7, 24

T

Taíno 10, 13, 15, 16, 18, 19, 20, 21, 22, 23 25

tobacco 23

Torres, Luis de 11

V

Venezuela 9, 11

Vespucci, Amerigo 29

voyages 8-9, 11